The Atlas of the Seven Continents™

ASIA
Wendy Vierow

The Rosen Publishing Group's
PowerKids Press™
New York

For Chris, who loves atlases

Published in 2004 by The Rosen Publishing Group, Inc.
29 East 21st Street, New York, NY 10010

First Edition

Editor: Frances E. Ruffin
Book Design: Maria E. Melendez
Book Layout: Eric DePalo

Photo Credits: Cover and title page, map of Asia, pp. 5, 10 © Earth Observatory/NASA; p. 7 © 2001 Todd Marshall; pp. 9, 11, 13, 19 © GeoAtlas; p. 15 illustrated by Eric DePalo; p. 17 (alligator, tiger) © Artville; p. 17 (panda) © Keren Su/CORBIS; p. 17 (bamboo) © Royalty-Free/CORBIS; p. 17 (snow monkeys) © Tom Brakefield/CORBIS; p. 19 (jeep factory) © Peter Turnley/CORBIS; p. 19 (rice fields) © Ron Watts/CORBIS; p. 19 (NASDAQ) © Hashimoto Noboru/Corbis Sygma; p. 21 (Hindu New Year Celebration) © David H. Wells/CORBIS; p. 21 (Muslim men) © Michael S. Yamashita/CORBIS; p. 21 (reading at the temple) © B.S.P.I./CORBIS; p. 21 (Jewish boy reading) © Dave Bartruff/CORBIS.

Vierow, Wendy.
Asia / Wendy Vierow.
    v. cm. — (The atlas of the seven continents)
Contents: Earth's continents and oceans — Asia long ago — How to read a map — Natural wonders of Asia — Countries of Asia — The climate of Asia — Asia's plants and animals — Making a living in Asia — The people of Asia — A scientist in Asia.
Includes bibliographical references and index.
ISBN 0-8239-6689-5 (library binding)
1. Asia—Geography—Juvenile literature. [1. Asia. 2. Asia–Maps.] I. Title.
DS5.92 .V54 2004
915—dc21

                                2002154696

Manufactured in the United States of America

Contents

Earth's Continents and Oceans

Asia is the largest continent on Earth. A continent is a large body of land. There are seven continents on Earth. They are Africa, Antarctica, Asia, Australia, Europe, North America, and South America. Some **geographers** believe that there are only six continents because Europe and Asia are not separated by water. Europe and Asia are sometimes called the continent of Eurasia. Earth also has four oceans. An ocean is a large body of salt water. Earth's oceans are the Arctic, Atlantic, Indian, and Pacific Oceans. Scientists think that, more than 200 million years ago, Earth's continents were all part of one giant continent. The continent was called Pangaea, and that Pangaea was surrounded by one ocean called Panthalassa. Over time Pangaea broke into smaller continents. This is because Earth's surface is always changing. Scientists think that the continents move because of Earth's **plates**. Earth's plates float on partly melted rock, deep inside Earth. When Earth's plates move, they cause changes on Earth's surface. The Himalaya Mountains in Asia were formed when two of Earth's plates pushed together.

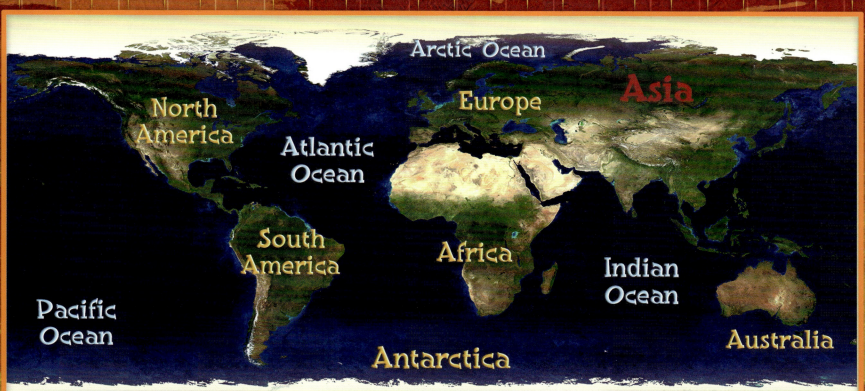

North America

Arctic Ocean

Europe

Asia

Atlantic Ocean

Pacific Ocean

South America

Africa

Indian Ocean

Australia

Antarctica

PERMIAN
286-245 million years ago

TRIASSIC
245-208 million years ago

JURASSIC
208-144 million years ago

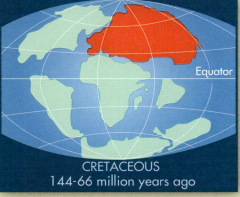

CRETACEOUS
144-66 million years ago

PRESENT DAY
From 66 million years ago

Top: This map of the world is a photo taken from high in the sky. The smaller maps show the giant continent Pangaea breaking up into smaller continents. One formed a landmass called Eurasia. Today we consider this mass of land to be two continents, Europe and Asia.

Dinosaurs and other animals lived in Asia during the Mesozoic era, about 245 million to 66 million years ago. The Mesozoic era is also called the Age of Dinosaurs because dinosaurs and other reptiles were the largest animals on Earth. Scientists know about life in Asia during the Mesozoic era by studying fossils, or the hardened parts of animals and plants that have died. During the Mesozoic era, the *Hybodus*, a shark, hunted for fish and reptiles in the water. Also in the water searching for fish were opthalmosaurs, reptiles that looked like porpoises. Opthalmosaurs' huge eyes, almost 10 inches (25 cm) across, helped them to see in dim light under water. In the air hunting for insects was the *Sordes*, a small pterosaur, or flying reptile. On the ground were huge meat-eating dinosaurs called yangchuanosaurs that grew up to 33 feet (10 m) long. In contrast, xiaosaurs were only about 5 feet (1.5 m) long and ate plants. Plants of the Mesozoic era included conifers, or trees with cones. Also included were cycads, or trees that looked like palms or ferns, and ginkgo trees. Flowering plants appeared in Asia during the Mesozoic era.

This drawing shows three tarbosaurs on a Chinese riverbank. Fossils of tarbosaurs have been found in Mongolia. These meat-eating dinosaurs lived about 74 million to 70 million years ago. At about 30 to 40 feet (9–12 m) long and weighing about 4 to 5 tons (7–8 t), tarbosaurs were close relatives of the tyrannosaurs that lived in North America.

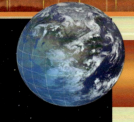

How to Read a Map

There are many different kinds of maps. Some maps, called physical maps, show different kinds of land and water in a place. Other maps, called political maps, show different countries or states in a place. You can find different maps in an atlas. Maps have different features that make them easier to read. The title of a map tells what the map shows. Often the title can be found in the map key or **legend**. If there are **symbols** on a map, such as a triangle for Mt. Everest, you can find out what they mean by looking at the map key or legend. The map scale shows how the size of a map compares to the actual size of a place. The compass rose, or north pointer, is a drawing on a map that shows direction. The four main directions on Earth are north, south, east, and west. North is the direction toward the North Pole. Latitude lines are lines on a map that run from east to west, and longitude lines run from north to south. The **equator** is 0° latitude, and the **prime meridian** is 0° longitude. Latitude and longitude lines make it easier to find places on a map. The equator runs through the country of Indonesia in the southern part of Asia.

ASIA: LANDMARKS

ARCTIC OCEAN

KARA SEA

LAPTEV SEA

Longitude Lines

Latitude Lines

BERING SEA

SEA OF OKHOTSK

CASPIAN SEA

YELLOW SEA

PACIFIC OCEAN

RED SEA

EAST CHINA SEA

ARABIAN SEA

PHILLIPPINE SEA

SOUTH CHINA SEA

N

EQUATOR

INDIAN OCEAN

ASIA
MERCATOR PROJECTION
0 km 500 1000 1500 km
scale at the Equator
GEOATLAS® · © 2001 Graphi-Ogre

MAP KEY ASIA: LANDMARKS

Angkor Wat	Taj Mahal	Mt. Everest	Dead Sea	Great Wall of China

Natural Wonders of Asia

This photograph of Japan was taken from space. It is possible to see snow on the mountains.

Asia has many kinds of **landforms**. It contains Mount Everest, which, at 29,028 feet (8,848 m), is the highest mountain on Earth. Mount Everest is part of the Himalayas, the world's highest mountain range. The Himalayas stretch from China to Afghanistan.

Asia also contains the lowest place in the world. The Dead Sea's shore is 1,312 feet (400 m) below **sea level**. The Dead Sea is located between the countries of Israel and Jordan. Deserts in Asia stretch from the Arabian **Peninsula** to the Gobi Desert in China and Mongolia. Northern Asia is a tundra, which is a cold, dry, desertlike place, where few things can exist. Asia's many islands and peninsulas form seas, including the Sea of Japan, the South China Sea, and the Andaman Sea. The Caspian Sea, which is actually a lake, is Earth's largest inland body of water at 143,550 square miles (371,793 sq km). The Yangtze in China is Asia's longest river at 3,915 miles (6,301 km).

ASIA: LAND AND WATER

KARA SEA

LAPTEV SEA

ARCTIC OCEAN

West
Siberian
Plain

CASPIAN SEA

SEA OF
OKHOTSK

BERING SEA

Plateau
of Tibet

SEA OF
JAPAN

PACIFIC
OCEAN

RED SEA

Persian Gulf

Gulf
of Oman

YELLOW
SEA

EAST
CHINA
SEA

Arabian
Peninsula

Bay
of Bengal

PHILIPPINE
SEA

ARABIAN
SEA

ANDAMAN
SEA

SOUTH
CHINA
SEA

INDIAN
OCEAN

EQUATOR

N

ASIA
MERCATOR PROJECTION
0 km   500   1000 1500 km
scale at the Equator
GEOATLAS® - © 2001 Graphi-Ogre

*This photo of the
Caspian Sea was
taken from space.*

*This photo of China's
Yangtze River was taken
from high above Earth.*

Countries of Asia

Asia has 47 countries, including Russia, a country that is part of the continents of Asia and Europe. Russia, the largest country in the world, is about twice the size of the United States. The largest country entirely in Asia is China at 3,705,820 square miles (9,598,030 sq km). With almost 1.3 billion people, China also has the largest population in the world. One of every five people on Earth is Chinese! The smallest country in Asia is Maldives at 115 square miles (298 sq km). About 275,000 people live there.

Some regions of Asia are known by different names. The Middle East includes countries in southwestern Asia, northern Africa, and southeastern Europe. Eastern Asia, sometimes referred to as the Far East, includes the countries of Cambodia, Laos, and Vietnam, which are east of the Indochina Peninsula. Countries in Asia have many different kinds of governments. China, with a population of more than one billion people, is the world's largest **communist** country. The one billion people in India live in the world's largest **democracy**. Some countries in Asia, such as Saudi Arabia, are ruled by kings.

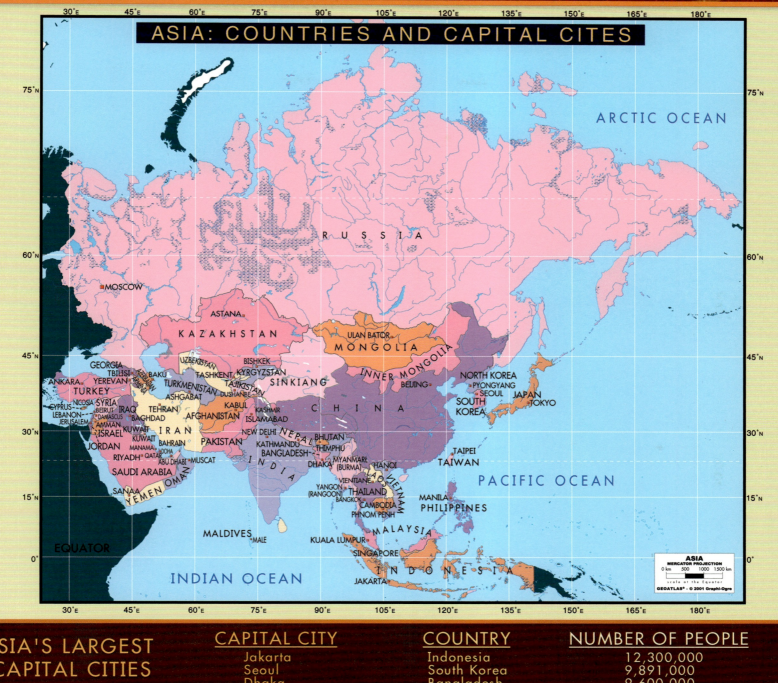

ASIA: COUNTRIES AND CAPITAL CITES

ARCTIC OCEAN

RUSSIA

MOSCOW

ASTANA

KAZAKHSTAN

ULAN BATOR

MONGOLIA

INNER MONGOLIA

GEORGIA
TBILISI
ANKARA
YEREVAN
TURKEY
BAKU
UZBEKISTAN
BISHKEK
TASHKENT
KYRGYZSTAN
TURKMENISTAN
TAJIKISTAN
SINKIANG
DUSHANBE
ASHGABAT

CYPRUS
NICOSIA
SYRIA
BEIRUT
LEBANON
DAMASCUS
JERUSALEM
IRAQ
BAGHDAD
TEHRAN
KABUL
AFGHANISTAN
KASHMIR
ISLAMABAD
CHINA

NORTH KOREA
PYONGYANG
SEOUL
SOUTH KOREA
JAPAN
TOKYO

BEIJING

AMMAN
ISRAEL
KUWAIT
JORDAN
MANAMA
BAHRAIN
RIYADH
QATAR
ABU DHABI
MUSCAT
IRAN
PAKISTAN
NEW DELHI
NEPAL
BHUTAN
KATHMANDU
THIMPHU
BANGLADESH
INDIA
DHAKA
MYANMAR
(BURMA)
HANOI
VIENTIANE
LAOS
VIETNAM
TAIPEI
TAIWAN

SAUDI ARABIA

SANAA
YEMEN
OMAN

YANGON
(RANGOON)
THAILAND
BANGKOK
CAMBODIA
PHNOM PENH
MANILA
PHILIPPINES

PACIFIC OCEAN

MALDIVES
MALE

KUALA LUMPUR
MALAYSIA

SINGAPORE

INDONESIA

JAKARTA

EQUATOR

INDIAN OCEAN

ASIA
MERCATOR PROJECTION
0 km   500   1000   1500 km
scale at the Equator
GEOATLAS® - © 2001 Graphi-Ogre

ASIA'S LARGEST CAPITAL CITIES

■ Capital Cities

CAPITAL CITY	COUNTRY	NUMBER OF PEOPLE
Jakarta	Indonesia	12,300,000
Seoul	South Korea	9,891,000
Dhaka	Bangladesh	9,600,000
Beijing	China	8,450,000
Moscow	Russia	8,369,200
Tokyo	Japan	8,130,000
Bangkok	Thailand	7,200,000
Tehran	Iran	6,758,845
Bagdad	Iraq	4,850,000
Singapore	Singapore	3,322,000

The Climate of Asia

Asia has many different climates. A climate is all the weather that occurs in one place over a long time. Asia's climates range from the cold, dry climate in the northern part of the continent to the hot, wet climate of countries near the equator. Climate includes temperature, or how hot or cold a place is. Climate also includes the amount of precipitation, or moisture that falls from the sky, such as rain or snow.

Many things can affect climate. In Asia the monsoon greatly affects climate. The monsoon is a great wind that blows over the Indian Ocean and onto the land. From April to October, the monsoon brings much rain and sometimes floods to southern Asia. From November to March, the monsoon blows from the northeast, causing cold, dry weather. Elevation, or how high a place is, also affects climate. In the mountains of Asia the climate is cold. In Asia's deserts, which are at lower elevations, the climate is often hot and dry. Latitude and moisture affect climate. Places closest to the equator are warm and wet. Malaysia and Indonesia have rain forests, or areas with warm, wet climates that lie near the equator.

ASIA: CLIMATE

Arctic Ocean

60°N

Pacific Ocean

SEA OF OKHOTSK

30°N

160°E

20°N

150°E

10°N

SOUTH CHINA SEA

Indian Ocean

Equator 0°

10°S 50°E

10°S

60°E 70°E 80°E 90°E 100°E

CLIMATE

- Tropical Wet
- Humid Subtropical
- Semiarid
- Arid
- Mediterranean
- Subtropical
- Highlands
- Warm Summer
- Cool Summer
- Subarctic
- Tundra
- ★ North Pole

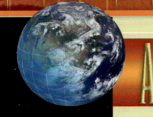

Asia's Plants and Animals

Asia has many different plants and animals. In the north live polar bears, arctic foxes, reindeer, and lemmings, which look like mice. In Russia, south of the Arctic Ocean, is Earth's largest fir and pine forest. Locusts, a kind of grasshopper, live in Mongolia and China and sometimes destroy entire fields of crops planted by farmers. Also in China are **endangered** giant pandas that live in bamboo forests. Silkworm mulberries also grow in China. People use the leaves of these trees to feed silkworms, which produce silk used to make cloth.

Nutmeg trees, rubber trees, teak trees, tea bushes, and bamboo grass grow in southern Asia. Animals living in southern Asia include antelopes, apes, monkeys, crocodiles, Indian elephants, leopards, rhinoceroses, scorpions, tigers, and cobras. The king cobra is the world's longest poisonous snake, up to 18 feet (5.5 m) long. Some king cobras have a head the size of a man's hand. Earth's largest lizard, the komodo dragon, lives in Indonesia. It can grow to more than 10 feet (3 m) long and weigh up to 300 pounds (136 kg).

Giant Panda

Japanese Snow Monkey

Bamboo

Siberian Tiger

Making a Living in Asia

Most Asians live near seacoasts or in river valleys where they can fish or farm. Asia leads the world in production of many crops. More than 90 percent of the world's rice is grown in Asia. Rice is an important food for many Asians as well as an important crop that farmers sell to other countries. Farmers also grow wheat to sell to other countries. India's farmers grow much of the world's sugarcane. Most of the world's teas also come from the Asian countries of China, India, Indonesia, and Sri Lanka. The world's leading producers of natural rubber are Indonesia, Malaysia, and Thailand. In places where people cannot grow crops, such as chilly northern Asia or the deserts of central Asia, some people raise sheep and cattle.

Much of the world's tin comes from southeast Asia. Most Asian countries do not have **industry.** However, there are factories in some countries, such as China, India, Israel, Japan, North Korea, Russia, Singapore, South Korea, Taiwan, and Turkey. Japan leads the world in making many products including automobiles, televisions, radios, computers, and electronics.

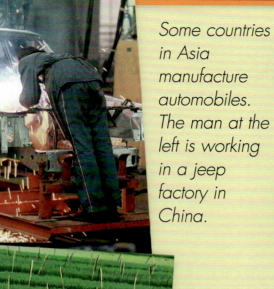

Some countries in Asia manufacture automobiles. The man at the left is working in a jeep factory in China.

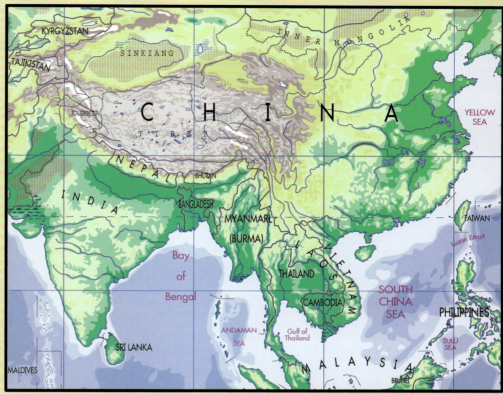

Middle: *This farmer is working in a flooded rice field in Yangzhou, China.*

Bottom: *The Japanese businessmen in this photo are attending a meeting at NASDAQ, a financial and business group.*

The People of Asia

Asia has more people than any other continent on Earth. About 60 percent of all people on Earth live in Asia. The people of Asia vary greatly. They speak many different languages, have different ways of life, and consist of different **ethnic groups**. The largest ethnic groups in Asia are the Chinese and the Arabs.

About 5,500 years ago, writing, law, and farming began in Asia. Most of the major religions practiced today began in Asia. These include **Buddhism**, **Christianity**, **Confucianism**, **Hinduism**, **Islam**, **Judaism**, **Shintoism**, and **Taoism**. Much of Asia's art has religious roots. The Taj Mahal, considered by many to be one of the world's most beautiful buildings, is an example of Islamic art. Hindus created temples, and Buddhists created many shrines, or special places where people go to pray. Asians also create other kinds of art, such as painting and sculpture. They also enjoy dance and theater.

Many of the world's major religions were started in Asia. These people are praying in different faiths, including Hinduism (top left), Shintoism (top right), Judaism (bottom right), and Islam (bottom left).

A Scientist in Asia

Asia holds many secrets to what life was like on Earth long ago. One kind of person who studies Earth's past is a paleontologist, or a person who studies dinosaurs. Paleontologist Dong Zhiming, who was born in China in 1937, has been interested in dinosaurs ever since he was a boy. In 1979, Dong found hundreds of dinosaur fossils at a construction **site** in Dashanpu, China. Dong wanted to save the fossils. He worked hard to get the government to stop the construction work. In 1980, the government agreed to protect the site. At the site were more than 100 dinosaurs, as well as the fossils of ancient fish, crocodiles, and pterodactyls, or flying reptiles. Dong thinks that the bones of so many different kinds of animals who lived in different times were in one place because of a huge flood. He believes the floodwaters washed the large animals into a lake that had fish and other water animals. Among Dong's famous discoveries are the yangchuanosaur found in 1978, and the xiaosaur in 1983. He still looks for and finds dinosaur fossils. He also talks to schoolchildren, hoping that they might become paleontologists.

Glossary

Buddhism (BOO-dih-zum) A faith based on the teachings of Buddha, started in India.

Christianity (kris-chee-A-nih-tee) A faith based on the teachings of Jesus Christ and the Bible.

communist (KOM-yuh-nist) Belonging to a system in which all the land, houses, and factories belong to the government and are shared by everyone.

Confucianism (kun-FYOO-shuh-nih-zum) A faith based on the teachings of Confucius, a Chinese man who lived from 551 B.C. to 479 B.C.

democracy (dih-MAH-kruh-see) A government that is run by the people who live under it.

endangered (en-DAYN-jerd) In danger of no longer existing.

equator (ih-KWAY-tur) An imaginary circle around the middle of Earth.

ethnic groups (ETH-nik GROOPS) Groups of people who have the same race, beliefs, practices, or language, or who belong to the same country.

geographers (jee-AH-gruh-ferz) Scientists who study the features of Earth.

Hinduism (HIN-doo-ih-zum) A faith that was started in India.

industry (IN-dus-tree) A moneymaking business in which many people work and make money producing a particular product.

Islam (IS-lom) A faith based on the teachings of Mohammed and the Koran.

Judaism (JOO-dee-ih-zum) The faith followed by Jews based on the Torah.

landforms (LAND-formz) Features on Earth's surface, such as hills or valleys.

legend (LEH-jend) A box on a map that tells what the figures on the map mean.

peninsula (peh-NIN-suh-luh) An area of land surrounded by water on three sides.

plates (PLAYTS) The moving pieces of Earth's crust, the top layer of Earth.

prime meridian (PRYM meh-RIH-dee-en) The imaginary line that passes through Greenwich, England, which is 0° longitude. Longitude is the distance east or west of the prime meridian.

sea level (SEE LEH-vul) The height of the top of the ocean.

Shintoism (SHIN-toh-ih-zm) A faith that is native to Japan.

site (SYT) The place where a certain event happens.

symbols (SIM-bulz) Objects or designs that stand for something else.

Taoism (DOW-ih-zum) A faith that follows the teachings of the sixth-century Chinese man Lao Tzu.

Index

Web Sites

Due to the changing nature of Internet links, PowerKids Press has developed an online list of Web sites related to the subject of this book. This site is updated regularly. Please use this link to access the list: www.powerkidslinks.com/asc/asia/